Clocks

CLOCKS

A QUANTUM BOOK

Published by Grange Books
an imprint of Grange Books Plc
The Grange
Kingsnorth Industrial Estate
Hoo, nr. Rochester
Kent ME3 9ND

1-84013-127-6

This book is produced by
Quantum Books Ltd
6 Blundell Street
London N7 9BH

Project Manager: Rebecca Kingsley
Project Editor: Judith Millidge
Designer: Wayne Humphries
Editor: Clare Haworth-Maden

The material in this publication previously appeared in
*Introduction to the Decorative Arts, Collector's Guide to
Clocks, Guide to Art Nouveau Style*

QUMTOCS
Set in Times
Reproduced in Singapore by Eray Scan Pte Ltd
Printed in Singapore by Star Standard Industries (Pte) Ltd

CONTENTS

INTRODUCTION

For thousands of years, time has fascinated people, and the history of measuring time goes as far back as pre-historic humans. In around 3,000 BC, the construction of Stonehenge was begun; by 1100 BC the task was left uncompleted. Through its six different phases of construction, the intentions of its builders changed, but at all times this stone circle was a calendrical instrument of remarkable precision.

Since that time, many ingenious inventions for marking the passage of time have been devised, but the culmination of these inventions is the clock. Not only are clocks practical, mechanical devices, but they often act as the centrepiece of a room, if not a whole house, and have frequently been made as objects of great art and beauty.

From their earliest days, humans, like most of the animal kingdom, have been aware of time, and have been able to estimate it quite accurately. With the growth of civilisation, however, our ability in this direction has gradually declined. As cultures developed, it became necessary to denote time in order, for example, to arrange meetings. The first method used on a daily basis was most likely the noting of the position of a shadow, such as one cast by a tree or a mountain. This obviously had its limitations, and as humans began to congregate in communities, shadow clocks, such as Cleopatra's Needle, were erected in market squares.

Opposite: The pyramids were used to mark the equinoxes.

Left: Cleopatra's Needle was built in Heliopolis in about 15 BC by Pharoah Thothmes III, and although it was a decorative and symbolic structure, it was also a giant sundial.

THE WOODEN SHADOW CLOCK

The next development was probably the small, portable, wooden shadow clock, which consisted of a horizontal bar with a raised crosspiece on one end. The shadow clock had to be placed facing east in the morning and west

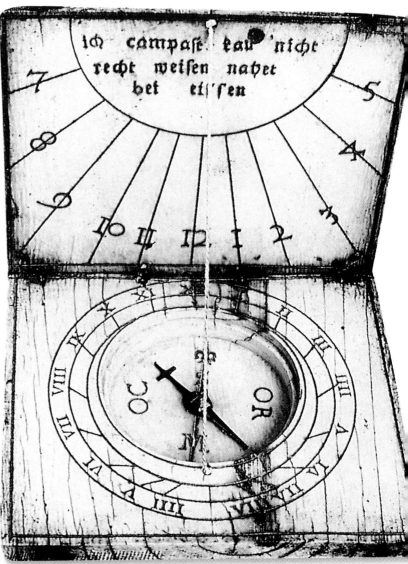

Above: The portable shadow clock was placed due east in the morning and west in the afternoon. The time was indicated by the shadow cast by the crossbar falling on the base, on which the hours were inscribed.

Right: A pocket sundial. Sundials are belived to have originated in Egypt.

in the afternoon, following the passage of the sun across the sky so that the crosspiece would cast a shadow along the horizontal bar. The final, and most popular, development of measuring time against the passage of the sun was the sundial. Still popular today as garden ornaments, the largest sundial in the world is to be found not in the ancient world, but in San Francisco, California. Dedicated in 1913, the gnomon (the pointer) is over 28 feet (8.5m) long and 17 feet (5.2m) high!

TEMPERATE CLIMATES

As methods of determining time, devices such as these were fine in sunny climates such as in the Middle East, one of the cradles of ancient civilisation. They are, however, far less practical in more temperate climates and are totally useless at night. To overcome this problem, various other forms of timekeepers, such as the sandglass, were devised. In a sandglass, time is measured by running sand through an opening from one container to another.

Devices such as this are still used today, but usually for small periods of time- one or two minutes – the length of time required either to soft- or hard-boil an egg.

Clepsydras, more commonly known as water clocks, are based on a similar principle. During the last millennium BC, water clocks were evolved by the Chinese, Egyptian and Greeks.

A set of four sandglasses, c. 1720. The studs on the frame indicate how long each glass takes to empty: one stud equals ¼ hour.

Fire clocks were also in common use. The most simple type of fire clock was probably a candle, which was graduated down its length in hours. In Britain, King Alfred (849–99), king of the West Saxons, was famous for his candle clock. Other similar timekeepers were based on the reduction of oil in a lamp, or the slow burning of powder along a grooved channel. The Japanese employed a similar device in their incense clocks.

THE MECHANICAL CLOCK

The birth of the mechanical clock, as it is known today, was made possible by the invention of the escapement mechanism. The earliest mechanical clock was completed in China in AD 725 by I Hsing and Liang Lingstan, but in the west the development was much later, and did not occur until the end of the

Above: The Dover Castle Clock, c. 1600, is one of the oldest clocks still to have its original verge escapement with foliot, from which the

regulating weights hang. The balance oscillates once every eight seconds, and the gearing is such that the great wheel rotates once an hour.

13th or the beginning of the 14th century. The verge-and-foliot escapement works on the principle of a vertical arbor or axle, on which a horizontally oscillating bar is mounted. Flags attached to the arbor alternately stop and release the teeth of a wheel, the escape wheel, with which other wheels and pinions engage that are used to indicate the time, usually by means of hands attached to them. One of the oldest examples in Europe of an original verge-and-foliot escapement is the Dover Castle Clock. Now in the Science Museum in London, the clock dates from around 1600, and in it the balance oscillates once every eight seconds, while the gearing is such that it allows the great wheel to rotate once every hour.

Many of the early clocks had no dial or hands, but merely struck the hours. Nearly all such clocks were made for ecclesiastical purposes, and the striking hours were thus used to summon the congregation to prayer. The oldest-surviving working clock in the world is the faceless clock dating from 1386, or possibly earlier, at Salisbury Cathedral in Wiltshire. Earlier dates, ranging back to around 1335, have been attributed to the weight-driven clock at Wells Cathedral, Somerset, but only the iron frame is original.

Domestic clocks

Domestic clocks did not come into use in England until around 1600, but yhey appeared far earlier on the Continent, particularly in southern Germany, around Augsburg and Nuremberg. The oldest examples were weight-driven wall clocks, the time measured almost

The ancient faceless clock in Salisbury Cathedral, Wiltshire.

11

German table clock, late 17th century. Clocks of this type were produced from the late 16th century until well into the 18th century. Measuring time of short duration and of considerable complexity, they sometimes featured an alarm and quarter-hour striking.

rather inaccurate timekeepers. It was only in around the year 1670, when the hairspring, used to control the balance, was invented that the performance of such timepieces was dramatically improved.

On most early turret clocks, the foliot controlled the timekeeping, with weights being moved, added to, or removed from, the bar to slow or speed it. On later domestic clocks, however, in particular the English lantern clocks that started to be produced in around 1600, a large balance wheel was preferred.

THE PENDULUM

A dramatic improvement in timekeeping took place in the mid-17th century as a result of the discovery of the pendulum. The artist Leonardo da Vinci (1452–1519) had made the observation in a cathedral that no matter how wide the arc of swing of a chandelier, the time it took to move from one side to the other was always the same. The physicist and astronomer Galileo (1564–1642) was later to prove that the length of the pendulum, not its amplitude (the maximum displacement from a zero value during one period of an oscillation), dictated the time of its swing. It was, however, left to Christiaan Huygens (1629–95), a Dutch mathematician, and Salomon Coster, an eminent Dutch clock-maker, to apply the pendulum principle to a clock. This they did in 1657, and in a very short time the idea had spread throughout Europe, and in particular to England.

Early pendulum clocks used a verge escapement: when the pendulum is at the extreme right of its swing, the front of two verge pallets is engaged with the vertical face of a 'scape wheel tooth. It is the tooth that gives the impulse to the pendulum. As the pendulum swings from right to left, the front pallet

always of a short duration, but the invention of the coiled spring in around 1500 enabled a whole range of spring-driven table clocks to be produced. These were much more portable than weight-driven wall clocks, and were often of great complexity. The introduction of the coiled spring was also to result in the birth of the watch.

The early watches and small spring clocks which employed a balance were, however,

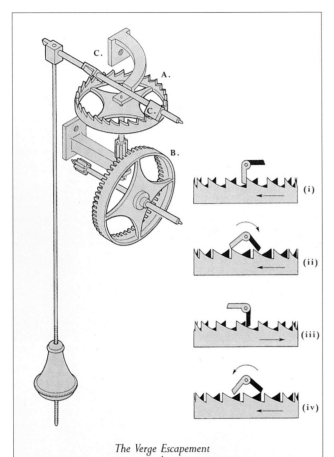

The Verge Escapement

1 When the pendulum is at the extreme right of its swing, the front of the two verge pallets is engaged with the vertical face of a 'scape wheel tooth. The tooth gives impulse to the pendulum through the pallet.

2 As the pendulum swings from right to left, the front pallet unlocks from the 'scape wheel.

3 The rear verge pallet now engages a tooth on the other side of the 'scape wheel; the momentum of the pendulum causes the 'scape wheel to recoil until the pendulum comes to rest at the left of its swing.

4 The sequence of events is then repeated, but with the pendulum swinging from left to right.

unlocks from the 'scape wheel, and the rear pallet engages a tooth on the other side of the wheel. The momentum of the pendulum causes the 'scape wheel to recoil until the pendulum comes to rest at the left of its swing. As the pendulum swings back to the right, the sequence of events is repeated.

PRECISION TIMEKEEPING

The quest for accurate timekeeping has been a dominant theme in life for at least the last millennium. The introduction of the pendulum in 1657 was closely followed by that of the anchor escapement. This escapement was simpler than the verge escapement, since no contrate wheel is required and the pallets are not directly connected to the pendulum. Some 12 years later, the royal, or seconds-beating, pendulum improved the accuracy of clocks from an error of maybe 5 to 10 minutes a day to 15 to 20 seconds a week.

A further advance was the introduction of maintaining power so that the clock did not stop when it was being wound. The first method devised was known as 'bolt and shutter', which was largely replaced in the 1730s by John Harrison's 'going ratchet'.

Another problem which became apparent as the accuracy of clocks increased, was the effect of changes in temperature. As the temperature rose, the pendulum rod would expand and increase in length, thus slowing the clock. To overcome this, two principle forms of compensated pendulum were invented: the mercury-compensated pendulum and the gridiron pendulum. In a mercury-compensated pendulum, a glass jar filled with mercury acts as the bob. As the rod expands down, the mercury expands up so that the effective length of the pendulum remains the same. The gridiron pendulum, on the other hand, involves

The verge escapement. The diagram shows the sequence of events in which the pendulum swings to the extreme right and the front of the two verge pallets is engaged with the vertical face of the 'scape wheel. The tooth gives the pendulum its impulse via the pallet. On the return swing, the front pallet is unlocked, the rear engaged and the 'scape wheel re-

the use of a pendulum rod consisting of rods of both brass and iron. These are joined in such a way that their expansions cancel each other out.

In around 1900, the problem of pendulum expansion was finally laid to rest with the use of a metal called invar, which has a negligible coefficient of expansion, and by the use of thermostats and electric heating devices to maintain precision clocks at a constant temperature. A further refinement was to enclose the clock movement in a sealed jar, which prevented it being affected by any changes in barometric pressure.

The final problem that had to be overcome on the mechanical clock – prior to its accuracy being vastly exceeded by atomic clocks – was how to prevent the movement from influencing the isochronicity – the regular or even beating of the pendulum. The ultimate solution took some 150 years to arrive at, and was achieved by Shortt, who devised a clock with two pendulums. One was the 'master', which was detached from the

Far right: An eight-day long-case regulator, Lecomber, Liverpool, c. 1820. The glazed door reveals the mercury-compensated pendulum. A high-grade regulator such as this would be capable of keeping time to within as great an accuracy as 1 to 2 seconds a week.

Thomas Tompion (1639–1713), the inventor of the year-duration clock.

movement and therefore swung freely, while the other was a 'slave', and had to do the work in the sense that it was attached to the movement. The subject of precision pendulum clocks is a vast and complex one. It stretches from Thomas Tompion's (1639–1713) famous year-duration clocks installed at the Royal Observatory at Greenwich in the 1670s to determine whether or not the earth rotated at a constant speed, right through to the precision machines of the 20th century. Widely regarded as the most accurate – and complicated – mechanical clock in the world is the

Olsen Clock, installed in the Town Hall in Copenhagen, Denmark. This clock, which has more than 14,000 units, took ten years to make, and the mechanism functions in no less than 570,000 different ways. The celestial-pole motion of the clock, which will take 25,743 years to complete a complete circle, is the slowest-moving designed mechanism in the world, and is accurate to 0.5 of a second in 300 years.

TIMEKEEPING AT SEA

By the early 18th century it was realised that accurate timekeeping at sea was essential for navigation and cartography. However, to make a clock that could tolerate the pitching and rolling of a ship at sea was a major undertaking, and one which demanded new technology that was beyond the skills of any of the clockmakers at that time.

To stimulate research, the British Admiralty formed a Board of Longitude, which was empowered to award a prize of up to £20,000 – a quite considerable sum in those days – to anyone who could devise a method of determining longitude at sea. In practice, this involved devising an accurate sea clock, and it was the dedication, determination and genius of one man, John Harrison (1693–1776), assisted in the early days by his brother James, who finally, over a period of some 40 years, overcame this problem. Harrison received the final part of his reward when he was nearly

A two-day chronometer, Brockbanks & Atkins, No 1159, London, c.,1890. This chronometer is suspended on gimbals in a brass-bound, three-tier mahogany box, typical of the hundreds of thousands of chronometers produced from c. 1820 to 1950, mostly in England, and used by navies around the world.

80 years old, but it was left to other men, such as John Arnold and Thomas Earnshaw, to make Harrison's invention a practical proposition. They simplified the clock's production so that it could be made in quantity without sacrificing any of its accuracy. The name now applied to these sea clocks is 'chronometers', and they are contained in three-tier wooden boxes and supported on brass gimbals. Whatever the movement of the ship, the gimbals ensure that the chronometer remains horizontal. To read the time, only the top lid needs to be lifted, so that the chronometer remains protected by the lower lid, which is glazed.

Above: John Harrison (1693–1776), who first invented an accurate sea clock.

Left: Two-day chronometer, Parkinson & Frodsham, Change Alley, London, No 3234, c. 1850.

LONGCASE
AND BRACKET CLOCKS

The invention of the pendulum in the mid-17th century gave rise to the longcase clock. Primarily, the longcase was a box to protect and conceal the relatively unsightly innards of weights, pulleys and lines or ropes. Pendulums used in conjunction with a verge escapement were short, averaging around 9 inches (23cm) in length, and had a wide arc of swing. Because the pendulum was short, it could therefore be accommodated within a narrow case, usually around 6 feet 3 inches (1.9m) high.

In keeping with the prevailing Puritan influence, the case was usually black and made either of ebony veneers or ebonised fruitwood.

THE ANCHOR ESCAPEMENT AND THE 'ROYAL' PENDULUM

To have had a longer pendulum would have made it impossible to confine it within the case and, moreover, it would have absorbed far more power. In around 1670, however, the anchor escapement was devised, and its invention is ascribed to William Clement. The basic difference between the anchor and the verge escapement, virtually universally used up until this time, is that the escape wheel is mounted parallel to all the other wheels in the clock and therefore no contrate wheel is required. It also needs a far narrower arc of swing, so that a much longer pendulum can be housed in a narrow case. This immediately made possible what was to become known as the 'royal' pendulum. This was approximately 3.28 feet (1m) in length and beat (moving from side to side) in exactly one second.

Far left and left: English longcase clock, probably by the Fromanteels, c. 1760–75; detail (left).

Previous page: English lacquer longcase clock, Henry Fish, London, c. 1720.

The principal advantages of these new developments were twofold: on the one hand the accuracy of clocks increased dramatically; and, on the other, the seconds could now be shown by a separate hand on the dial, directly connected to the arbor (axle) on which the pallets were mounted.

MAINTAINING POWER

Following William Clement's invention of the anchor escapement in 1670, there were to be no major advances in the design of the mechanical components of longcase clocks for the next 250 years. One improvement introduced into the construction of the longcase clock was 'maintaining power' – keeping the clock going while it was being wound up. This was achieved by the introduction of an auxiliary spring that ensured that the power was removed from the train of wheels during winding. The first form was known as 'bolt and shutter', whereby shutters covered the winding holes and could only be removed by pulling a cord or depressing a lever. This action also charged a spring-loaded bolt, which pressed onto one of the wheels in the clock and kept it going.

This form of maintaining power gave considerable trouble, and by the early 1700s its use was largely discontinued when a more efficient method of maintaining power, the 'going ratchet', was devised by John Harrison

Left: English longcase clock by Daniel Delander, London, c. 1715. An example of the high-quality pieces that were being produced in the first part of the 18th century.

Right: English longcase clock, Edward East, London, c. 1680.

Far right: English longcase clock by William Speakman, London, c. 1685. A fine example of walnut and olivewood veneer parquetry.

Right: The 10 inch (25.4cm) square dial has the largest form of cherub spandrels, a narrow seconds ring, and a cut-out for the central alarm disc and date aperture, directly above 6 o'clock.

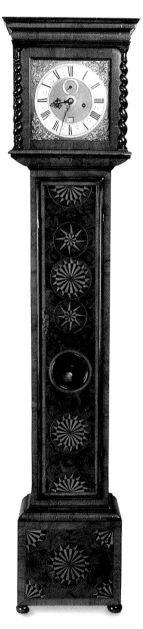

in the 1720s. In many clocks, the 'bolt and shutter' mechanism was removed and replaced with Harrison's going ratchet, and where the originals are seen, they are generally, however, reinstatements.

THE DIAL

The earliest longcase clocks were small, usually no more than 6 feet 4 inches (1.9m) in height. Yet as the 17th century progressed, these longcases gradually got taller, averaging about 7 feet (2.1m) without a caddy, and 7 feet 5 inches (2.26m) with one, by around 1700. At the same time, the dials, which were always square, also got larger. In the early days they were around 10 inches (25.4cm). They grew to 11 inches (28cm) and eventually to 12 inches (30.5cm), the size that was to become by far the most popular for the rest of the life of the longcase clock.

Between around 1710 and 1715, a major change occurred: to the top of the square dial, an arch was added. This gave additional space on which to place various information, such as a name plaque, a strike/silent regulation, or calendar work. While at least 95 per cent of the clocks made in London after this time employed the 'breakarch', the square dial never went entirely out of fashion, particularly in the more rural areas, where it continued to be used well into the 19th century.

CASE STYLES

Once ebony had gone out of fashion, the most popular wood for veneering clock cases in London was walnut, both highly figured and relatively plain. Outside the capital, in the country, oak continued to remain the popular choice for clock cases.

By the 1760s, as the austere influence and taste of the Puritans declined, the black ebonised cases began to give way to cases veneered in woods such as walnut and olive, and it was not long before these were decorated, firstly with parquetry, which is formed from geometric designs let into the case, and subsequently with marquetry, usually of floral and bird designs.

At first, marquetry decoration was confined to panels laid on the base and the trunk door. Gradually, however, the decoration spread to the hood and to most of the case. Towards the end of the 17th century, the floral patterns began to give way to arabesques composed of bold, contrasting strapwork, usually of dark wood laid on a light background, and frequently incorporating motifs of figures, birds and butterflies. The final development of marquetry, known as 'seaweed', consists of very fine, delicate tracery, usually employing only two different types of wood.

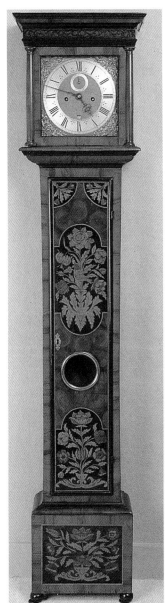

Above and right: English floral marquetry on a longcase clock, 1695. Floral marquetry followed hard on the heels of the geometric patterns of parquetry. At first its use was confined to panels on the trunk and base of the clock, but it rapidly spread to the hood, and was eventually to be laid all over the clock, not just in the panels.

Although the technique of marquetry developed roughly in the order described, there were nevertheless overlaps of style. It was by no means unusual to see floral marquetry in use as late as 1710, and it even enjoyed a brief revival in the Victorian and Edwardian eras of the late 19th and early 20th centuries. However, at roughly the time that the 'breakarch'-dial style came into favour, the use of marquetry went out of fashion.

'CHINOISERIE' OR LACQUERWORK

This is the decoration of furniture and other objects with gilded gesso (a form of plasterwork), which is laid on a 'japanned' or hand-coloured lacquered background. Its use in the Far East goes back at least 2,000 years, but it only appeared in Europe following increased contact and trade with the Orient in the 15th century. It arrived first in Venice and Genoa, then Portugal and finally, some 200 years later, in The Netherlands and England. In the early 1600s, small pieces of lacquerwork, such as tea caddies were imported, but later, larger items, such as wall panels, were shipped back to the rast for lacquering. It was, however, rare for large pieces of furniture to be imported, and the number of pieces sent out to the Orient for decoration was very small.

Lacquer decoration first began to be used on furniture in The Netherlands in around 1660 – somewhat later in England – and it was probably never used on clock cases until after 1690. A considerable number of lacquer clocks were produced in the period 1710–30, but it never completely went out of fashion. Under influential cabinetmakers such as Chippendale in the third quarter of the 18th century, there

English lacquer longcase clock, Henry Fish, London, c. 1720.

was a renewed and considerable vogue for lacquered decoration. The most common colour was black, but various forms of red, tortoiseshell and green were also used. Rarely seen, however, on these clocks, is white.

MAHOGANY

The 1720s witnessed a decline in the popularity of walnut furniture, which was the inevitable result of a combination of factors. Firstly, walnut was in short supply, largely due to the loss of trees due to disease. In France, the situation became so serious that the export of walnut was banned. Secondly, following Britain's rapidly growing trade in the West Indies and America, there was an increase in the amount of mahogany imported, mainly from Cuba and Honduras. Mahogany was an ideal wood for cabinetmaking: unlike walnut, it was not subject to attack by worms; it was available in long, wide boards; and it could also be obtained as highly figured, and such natural patterning made it perfect for veneers.

The earliest mahogany clock cases, however, tended not to be of highly figured wood, but by 1765 to 1785 cases of the highest quality, with superb veneers, were being produced. By the end of the century, only a handful of longcase clocks were still being produced in London, and those made during the Regency period tended to have circular dials, either painted or of silvered brass.

COUNTRY LONGCASE CLOCKS

While the clocks produced in London tended to be standardised in design, those made outside the capital showed far more individuality, and frequently regional characteristics developed. For instance, in the West Country, as befits a seafaring area, clocks frequently

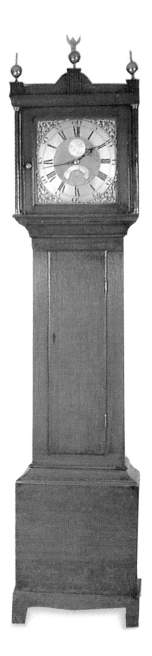

featured rolling moon discs in the arch, with ships, and often showed the time of high water at a particular port. A wavy border was sometimes a part of the inner aspect of the hood door, and rope-twist columns were also popular decorative devices.

When the town where the clock was made was close to London, then the influence of the London designs was more obvious. In more remote areas, entirely different designs evolved, for example, the swan-neck pediment. While immensely popular in country-made clocks, the device is rarely to be found on London-made clocks.

THIRTY-HOUR CLOCKS

The term 'thirty hour' really implies that a clock will run a little more than a day, so that if you were to wind it a few hours later than usual it would not stop. Very few were made in London, but they were particularly popular in the country districts because of their small size – usually less than 6.5 feet (1.98m) tall, to suit the low ceilings of the owners' homes – and relatively affordable in cost.

Up until around 1770, thirty-hour clocks usually had solid-oak cases and a square brass dial, frequently of 10 inches (25.4cm), but on later clocks both 11 inches (28cm) and 12 inches (30.5cm) square. The early clocks only had one hand – no minutes were indicated – and virtually all thirty-hour clocks were driven by a single weight that was rewound every day by pulling down on a rope or chain. The advantage to this was that maintaining power

Left: English pagoda-topped longcase clock, John Monkhouse, London, c. 1770.

Right: English thirty-hour, longcase clock, George Donisthorpe, Birmingham, c. 1780.

was provided – that is, the clock was kept going during the rewinding, and no winding holes were required in the dial.

Towards the end of the 18th century, mahogany cases were used far more frequently, and usually in conjunction with a painted dial. But by this time the thirty-hour clocks were in decline in favor of eight-day clocks.

WHITE- OR PAINTED-DIAL LONGCASE CLOCKS

Once again, few painted-dial clocks were made in London, but from 1780 they were very popular elsewhere in the country, and before the century was out they were probably outselling brass-dial clocks at a rate of ten to one.

The first-recorded reference to white dials was discovered by Brian Loomes and appeared in the *Birmingham Gazette* in 1772. It read:

> *Osborne and Wilson,
> manufacturers of white clock dials
> in imitation enamel, in a manner
> entirely new, have opened a
> warehouse at No. 3 in Colmore Row,
> Birmingham. Where they have an
> assortment of the above mentioned
> goods. Those who favour them with
> orders may depend upon their being
> executed with the utmost punctuality
> and expedition.*

The earliest white dials often had no decoration other than the numerals and the signature, or perhaps spandrels in the form of raised gilt decoration in the four corners. Nevertheless, they rapidly became more colourful, and typically displayed flowers such as roses and peonies in the corners, and in the arch if there was no moon disc. If there was a moon disc and the clock was made near the coast, especially in the West Country, then ships

were a common feature of the decoration. Inland, buildings were chosen as part of the subject, but a popular feature was to illustrate the four seasons by means of flowers, crops, or country girls dressed in suitable costumes or carrying out activities associated with the different times of year.

As the 19th century progressed, the decoration on the dial increased. The corners were filled in solidly and scenes and people were depicted in the arch. Indeed, by the 1850s, shortly before the demise of the longcase clock, virtually the whole of the dial was covered with decoration, in a style typical of Victorian *horror vacuii*.

Left and below: English white-painted-dial longcase clock, John Chapman, Loughborough, c. 1790.

COMPLEX CLOCKS

Between 1720 and 1780 a considerable number of complex clocks were made. Some of these chimed the quarter hour, usually on eight bells, while others would play a tune, either every one or three hours – or at will! Others still gave complex astrological information.

But a further complexity added to a clock's design was to make it run for longer than one week. A month was the period most often chosen, and from 1670 to 1710 this duration was the most popular. Nevertheless, clocks with three, six and even twelve months' running duration were also being made.

FRENCH LONGCASE CLOCKS

Virtually no longcase clocks – in the English sense of the term – were produced in France,

Above and left: English quarter-chiming and tidal-dial longcase clock with year calendar, by Charles Clay, London, c. 1725. A fine-quality longcase clock by a maker who is famous for his musical, in particular, organ, clocks.

Above: English astronomical longcase clock by Edward Cockey, Warminster, c. 1710. A remarkable example of country clockmaking. The superb-quality craftsmanship and artistry of the early clockmakers set a standard seldom equalled as the 18th century progressed.

but the French did make clocks that resembled English models in some way. In the 18th century, for example, the French sometimes placed their clocks on decorative matching pillars, which, in effect, gave them roughly the same height and width as a longcase clock. From 1760 onwards, the French also housed their regulators in far more restrained, one-piece cases of superb quality which, by 1780 to 1810, were often free of all ornamentation.

What might be called longcases were made in the country districts of France in the 19th century to house what were known as 'Comtoise' clocks – clocks made in the district of Franche-Comté. These usually had ornamental, thin-pressed brass dials, often with enamelled centres, and frequently very large and decorative pendulums. Most often, the cases were made of woods native to the region, such as cherry, apple or pine. A characteristic feature of these clocks was that they struck at the hour and repeated it again at two minutes past.

THE AMERICAN LONGCASE CLOCK

The earliest clocks to appear in the New World were undoubtedly those brought over by the first settlers, and it is likely that these were relatively small clocks, such as lanterns, not longcase clocks, which would have been difficult and expensive to transport. But among the settlers were an increasing number of blacksmiths and clockmakers, and one of the first-recorded craftsmen, Abel Cottey (died 1717), emigrated from Crediton in Devon in 1682 to

Tall clock by Isaac Brokaw, Bridge Town, New Jersey, c. 1810. The Federal case of this clock, made of, and veneered in, mahogany, is typical of east New Jersey's finest cabinetmakers.

Philadelphia, where he is known to have prospered and made longcase clocks – or tall-case clocks, as they are called in the United States.

By the early 18th century, clockmaking was fairly well established in New York, New England, Virginia and Pennsylvania, and was carried out in much the same way as back in England at that time. As the century progressed, clockmaking gradually spread to other areas, and certain places, such as Connecticut, became important centres for the craft.

The basic methods of construction in America were similar to those used in England, but they often had to be adapted to suit local needs. Often there was a lack of suitable materials: brass was in short supply, and to overcome this problem the metal was used in strip form, or wood was used as a substitute. Similarly, local wood, such as cherry, was often used for the cases.

Although some complete longcase clocks were obviously imported, in the majority of instances it was more likely that the movement were bought in, complete with dials, and the cases manufactured locally. A great number of components were also imported – sometimes entire movements and dials, at other times just wheels, pinions, barrels, plates, hands or pendulum bobs.

Before the War of Independence, a fairly small, but gradually increasing, number of tall-case clocks were being produced. By the early 19th century, the first examples of smaller, mass-produced clocks were starting to appear. In 1802 the Willards of Massachusetts evolved their own style of case and movement – weight driven with an anchor escapement and pendulum mounted in the front – in the guise of the 'banjo clock', so-called because of its shape. These are still made today.

While Gideon Roberts in Bristol,

Connecticut, produced wall clocks with wooden movements, it is Eli Terry of Connecticut who is credited with making the first mass-produced clocks in 1806, when he filled an order for 4,000 thirty-hour wooden movements, dials, hands, pendulums and weights for Levi and Edward Porter of Waterbury. Subsequently known as the Porter Contract, the order was completed in 1810. Delivery of such a huge number of clocks was made possible by the complete interchangeability of all the components, something that had not been attempted before and, indeed, signalled the birth of mass production. Eli Terry's contract gave rise to some 200 manufacturers in western Connecticut, making hundreds of thousands of clocks each year, all using similar wooden movements to those devised by Terry. This continued until the 1830s, when readily available, rolled brass replaced the wood.

THE DUTCH LONGCASE CLOCK

As in England, the production of longcase clocks in The Netherlands began shortly after the invention of the pendulum, and the early Dutch clocks usually had a walnut case of simple, pleasing proportions resting on bun feet. No more than 7 feet (2.13m) in height, they often had spiral-twist columns on the hood and were surmounted by carved decoration that was frequently quite elaborate. The square dials of the clocks often had an iron, velvet-covered plate onto which the raised chapter ring and the spandrels were then applied. To

Left: American tall-case clock by Aaron Willard, Boston, c. 1800.

Right: Tall clock, Isaac Brokaw, Bridge Town, New Jersey, c. 1810.

contrast with the black velvet, ornamental gilt-brass hands were used. By the end of the 18th century, the arched dial had also been adopted, often with moon phases, and the clocks became much taller, frequently employing a *bombe* base.

Dutch striking, in which the clock strikes out the hours in full, both at the half-hour on a high bell and on the hour on a lower-tuned bell, was usually a feature of Dutch longcase design, and often an alarm was also incorporated. Made in substantial numbers were musical clocks. These were usually tall and often quite complex, for example, with large apertures at the centre of the dial for the days of the week and the months of the year, which were often represented by paintings or engravings of deities and zodiacal signs. A characteristic feature of many of the most elaborate clocks – which could be up to 11 feet (3.35m) tall – was the mounting on the top of the case of one or more figures, the most popular being Atlas supporting the world on his shoulders.

In contrast to England, where the popularity and production of longcase clocks rapidly increased as the 18th century progressed, in The Netherlands during the same period wall clocks were in greater demand, and the production of longcase clocks declined.

BRACKET CLOCKS

The term 'bracket clock', although in general use, is somewhat confusing, since in the vast majority of instances such clocks did not in fact rest on brackets, but were far more likely to have been placed on a table, sideboard or mantelpiece. An alternative name, and one more commonly used in the 17th century, is 'spring clock', but even that term can

now be equally well applied to spring-driven wall clocks.

Bracket clocks, like longcase clocks, started to be made shortly after the invention of the pendulum. However, where the longcase clock rapidly adopted the anchor escapement devised in 1675, with its long, seconds-beating pendulum, this was of less advantage to the bracket clock – indeed, it was a positive disadvantage, in that it made the escapement

Left and above: Dutch longcase clock by Jan Van Der Swelling, Leiden c. 1770. A Dutch longcase clock of a style usually made in Amsterdam during the 18th century.

far more critical and the clock more difficult to set up. Furthermore, portability, which was of no importance in a longcase clock, was a major factor with a bracket clock. Clocks with verge escapements are much more tolerant of being off-level and thus out of beat. It was only around 1800 that the changeover from verge to anchor escapement took place in bracket clocks.

As with the longcase clocks, the early bracket clocks were architectural in style, and ebonised. By the 1670s a few were beginning to be veneered in walnut or olivewood, but ebony continued to dominate, and because of their small size bracket clocks seldom featured marquetry decoration, although some did use lacquer decoration.

Between 1675 and 1680 the architectural style began to give way to the caddy top, which

was either left plain or decorated with fretted and gilt-brass mounts. By 1685, the fretted-out, gilt-brass basket top was being employed. Often this was cast, but more frequently the designs featured on it were created by *repoussé* (beaten-out) work. The earliest of these were relatively small and shallow, but gradually they got larger and increasingly more elaborate – so much so that by 1710 a double-basket top was often favoured. The majority of these clocks continued to be ebony veneered, with only rare models finished in walnut, olivewood or other, similar types of wood.

By 1715 the breakarch dial had come into fashion, and in its early stages was relatively shallow. The caddy top eventually gave way to the inverted bell, a style that was to persist until the middle of the 18th century. Once again, the vast majority of these clocks were black, but they were usually now veneered in ebonised fruitwood rather than ebony. By the 1760s the inverted bell top had been superseded by the bell top, and other case designs evolved. It was at this time that mahogany became favoured for bracket-clock cases.

Up until this time, the brass dial incorporating a raised chapter ring and spandrels had always been used, but by the 1770s the all-over engraved and silvered-brass dial was to be frequently seen. Also increasingly popular from the 1780s onwards was the painted or white dial, but it was usually left plain, with no decorations at the corners. This was largely due to the fact that the majority of bracket clocks being produced at the time originated in London. It was principally in the country that white dials carried coloured decorations, although this is by no means always true.

By the 1800s painted, and occasionally silvered-brass, dials were being used almost universally on bracket clocks. The earlier ones,

Lef: Spring clock by John Drew, London, late 17th century. The glazed sides and back door reveal the twin fusee movement, with its engraved backplate.

Below: Table clock by Robert Seignior, London, c. 1765. Early spring-driven clocks were architectural in style, and usually veneered in ebony or sometimes walnut or olivewood, and bore a resemblance to longcase clocks.

usually just prior to 1800, were breakarch in form, but after this time they were generally circular in shape.

During the Regency period, several new case styles evolved, which persisted in gradually modified forms until the middle of the century and often incorporated inlaid brass. During the Victorian and Edwardian eras, clocks tended to be larger and were also more elaborately

Left and above: Spring clock by Robert Halsted, London. Halsted was apprenticed in 1662 and became a freeman of the Clockmaker's Company in 1668, rising to become master of the company in 1699. The two-train movement of this clock has a verge escapement, pull-quarter repeat on three bells, engraved backplate, a back cock cover and external clickwork. The ebony-veneered case has a repoussé *basket top decorated with cherubs.*

decorated, sometimes with carving. Initially the white dial predominated, but from around 1870 onwards reproductions of Georgian clocks became popular, copying their predecessor's styles, sometimes being smaller but frequently being much larger. In these latter cases, the larger size accommodated a nest of bells or gongs to allow quarter-chiming, which had become extremely popular following the completion of the great clock at Westminster,

Above: Bracket clock, William Webster, London, c. 1775.

Right: Bracket clock, Andrew Dickie, Edinburgh, 1736–52.

now commonly referred to as 'Big Ben', although the name in fact belongs to the bell.

As the century progressed, increasingly chiming was provided by a series of coiled gongs: four for Westminster, eight for other chimes, such as St Michael. Gongs were also used more and more for the hour strike, even when bells were used for the quarter. Possibly the ultimate was the clock that produced one or two different tunes on eight, nine or even ten bells, and could also provide Westminster chimes on four gongs with a gong for the hour.

By the early 20th century, the production of clocks such as these and, indeed, of most bracket clocks, had virtually ceased in the United Kingdom. They were largely superseded by smaller and cheaper French and German copies of earlier English bracket-clock styles, and by the very decorative French mantel clocks.

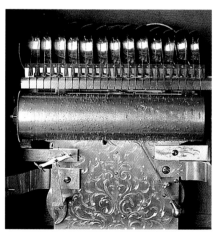

Above and left: Musical clock, Adam Travers, Liverpool, c. 1790. The detail shows the 12-tune musical movement.

WALL AND SHELF CLOCKS

In England the longcase clock was to dominate clock production from the time of the invention of the pendulum in 1657. However, the earliest wall clock was undoubtedly the lantern clock which first appeared in Europe, particularly in southern Germany and northern Italy in around 1500, with production beginning in England about one hundred years later.

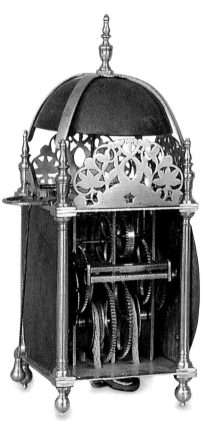

Previous page: English tavern, or Act of Parliament, clock, William Nash, Bridge, c. 1780.

Above and above left: Verge lantern clock by Thomas Palmer, Shefford, late 17th century. This lantern clock has a short bob pendulum with a verge escapement.

LANTERN CLOCKS

Lantern clocks were sometimes hung on a wall by means of a hoop extending backwards from the top plate of the movement and engaging on a suitable hook. At the same time, spikes fixed to the rear of the back feet were pushed into the wall to keep the clock vertical and to stop it from moving while it was being wound. From this is derived the term 'hoop and spikes', but alternatively a bracket, usually of oak, was fixed to the wall and the clock rested on this. The first lantern clocks made in Germany employed a verge escapement with a foliot, but this gradually gave way to the balance wheel, which was used on virtually all early English lantern clocks.

With the discovery of the pendulum in 1657, the balance wheel was to become obsolete, and most of the clocks that had been made with a balance wheel were subsequently converted to pendulums, which provided far more accurate timekeeping.

Some 12 years later, the anchor escapement, usually employed in conjunction with the 39 inch (1m) seconds-beating pendulum, was invented. However, whereas with the longcase clock the changeover from verge to anchor escapement was almost instantaneous, with the lantern clock the change occurred only gradually, over a period of perhaps 30 or 40 years. This was in part due to the fact that the lantern clocks were relatively simple and inexpensive: with only one hand to mark the hours, they were never expected to keep really accurate time.

By around 1720, the heyday of the lantern clock was largely over, and it was almost completely supplanted by the longcase clock, especially the thirty-hour version. Nevertheless, the production of lantern clocks in the 18th century never completely ceased.

FRENCH AND SWISS WALL CLOCKS

During the 18th and 19th centuries the French produced two types of wall clocks, both of which they termed' cartel clocks'. However, the term' cartel clocks' is now usually reserved as a description for decorative wall clocks, while the second type is usually referred to as 'bracket clock on bracket', since the two components are usually entirely separate from each other. In France, several terms have been used to describe the bracket on which the clocks rested: *soubassement, console, support* and *cul de lampe*. The word *socle* is also sometimes used, but this is better confined to describing the plinth on which a clock rests.

CARTEL CLOCKS

Cartel clocks, which are nearly always of fire-gilt bronze, and usually beautifully chased and decorated, started to be produced in the early 18th century, and the first clocks had fairly substantial movements with rectangular plates, silk suspensions, verge escapements and fine, convex, enamel dials. Frequently they were signed on the dial and on the back plate.

These clocks continued to be made in gradually changing form until the beginning of the 19th century, when the mass production of French clock movements – which were still of very high quality – started in earnest. These mass-produced versions were smaller than their predecessors, and had circular plates, usually with an anchor escapement and either a countwheel or rack strike in place of the earlier silk suspension.

On the whole, the clocks became smaller in size, and they maintained their popularity throughout the 19th century – they were still being made right up until the outbreak of World War I. Nevertheless, they were never produced in the same quantities as mantel clocks.

Left: Lantern clock by George Thatcher, Cranbrook, 18th century. By around 1700 the majority of lantern clocks employed the anchor escapement, together with a long pendulum. Many of the clocks were fixed to the wall by a hoop attached to the top plate of the movement, together with spikes fitted into the back of the rear ball feet. In other cases, such as this example, a simple oak bracket was used.

Above: Weight-driven lantern clock converted to spring, Barnard Dammant.

FRENCH MANTEL CLOCKS

In the last half of the 17th and the first half of the 18th centuries in France, the approach to clockmaking was vastly different to that in England. Except for those clocks made in the very early period, French clocks were far more ornate and, indeed, this aspect of their design was usually the dominant factor. And whereas in England clockmaking usually only required two craftsmen – the clockmaker and the cabinetmaker – in France far more people were involved: often a sculptor, caster, chaser, engraver, gilder, enameller and porcelain manufacturer might all be involved in the creation of a clock. The better clocks were often considered works of art, and many fine artists were employed to produce designs for mounts for cases, or even entire cases. This is not surprising in a country that produced some of the best bronzes in the world, most of the subjects for which came from mythology.

The decoration applied to the clock cases varied: tortoiseshell was often used extensively,

Left: Gilt-bronze cartel clock by Martinet, early 18th century. The French timepiece of fire-gilt bronze features a convex, enamelled dial, verge escapement and pull-quarter repeat on two bells. Signed 'London' on the dial, because part of the Martinet family came to England as refugees in the early 18th century, the clock would nevertheless have been manufactured in France.

Below: Mantel clock, late 18th century. In this fine-quality, fire-gilt and bronze mantel clock, the figure of Astronomy reads a book while another volume rests at her feet. Cupid sits amid a globe and other astronomical instruments.

either on its own or in combination with in-laid brass, called *boulle* work, after the inventor of the process. Often silver would be let into the tortoiseshell, and horn, usually stained green, would be used as a veneer.

Beautifully conceived and executed porcelain clocks were produced quite early in the 18th century; the cases were often imported from the famous factories of Meissen and Dresden, and frequently comprised flowers and figures of young girls. Fine bronze models of animals – lions, elephants and horses – were used to carry the clock itself, or the figure of Chronos carried the clock under his arm.

BRACKET CLOCK ON BRACKET

These clocks started to be produced in around the beginning of the 18th century, and were usually, but by no means always, large clocks of anything up to 5 feet (1.52m) in length. The clock and its bracket, although separate pieces, were always conceived as one overall design, and were usually highly decorative. The pendulum was frequently visible, and the dial had an ornamental background on which raised enamel numerals were placed.

The most common decoration applied to the case was of *boulle* marquetry, that is, delicate designs in brass let into a tortoiseshell background. Tortoiseshell was also used alone, usually stained brown or green, with the addition of ormolu (gilded brass or bronze) mounts or lacquer decoration.

DUTCH WALL CLOCKS

While longcase clocks were to dominate production in England from the mid-17th century, in The Netherlands the simple, rectangular wall clock, which hung from the wall by two eyelets, appeared on the scene. These were generally known as 'Hague' clocks, and the

Musical clock by Jacquet Droz, c. 1770. A fine red boulle *pendule complete with original bracket. Signed Pierre Jacquet Droz, the most eminent of all Swiss clockmakers who worked in La Chaux de Fonds, he specialised in musical clocks, including those incorporating singing birds.*

earliest examples were just timepieces, that is to say, they had no strike. Probably because Christiaan Huygens, who had invented the pendulum, had visited Paris regularly, clocks very similar to the Hague clocks appeared in the French capital at almost the same time as they appeared in The Netherlands.

As the century progressed, these clocks gradually became more ornate. Either spring or weight driven, of single- or eight-day duration, strike work and an alarm were also often provided. For the pendulum, silk suspension was often employed, and the dial usually consisted of a velvet-covered, cast-iron plate, onto which a silver or silvered chapter ring was mounted. Sometimes this was solid, at other times it would be fretted out.

THE *STOELKLOK*

The *stoelklok* is basically a clock resting on a wall bracket, and it may be either very simple in design, as with the very early clocks and similar to the lantern clocks, or extremely ornate, as are most of the examples from the 19th century. The *stoelklok,* along with the *staartklok* (tail clock) were to dominate Dutch clock production during the late 17th and 18th centuries. In contrast, in England, the production of these types of clocks was very small compared to that of longcase clocks.

The first of the *stoelkloks* produced – examples of which are now exceedingly rare – employed a balance wheel and verge escapement, but the vast majority did in fact make use of a pendulum. The earliest clocks also often had a raised chapter ring laid on a plain background, but within a short period the entire dial would become decorated with painted scenes.

Although the first examples of these clocks were made in and around Amsterdam, their production rapidly spread throughout much

of the country, and distinct, regional differences evolved. In later clocks, iron or lead decoration was often added, sometimes in the form of cherubs, female figures or animals, while painted wooden figures, usually mermaids, were added to either side of the bracket at the back.

THE *STAARTKLOK*

The *staartklok* is really a hooded wall clock, and it is likely that these evolved from the earliest of these clocks produced in England or The Netherlands. The characteristic feature of the *staartklok*, however, is the extension of the bracket down below the clock – in effect,

Left: Stoelklok, c. 1740. *Probably made in Friesland, in the north-eastern part of the country, in around 1740, this* stoelklok *has so-called 'ears' on either side of the back of the case, and its frets are made of lead. The dial and the stool on which the clock rests are painted.*

Below: Stoelklok, c. 1800. *Note the very ornate nature of the movement, with attractively turned vertical and horizontal pillars and verge escapement. It is of a thirty-hour duration and has an alarm.*

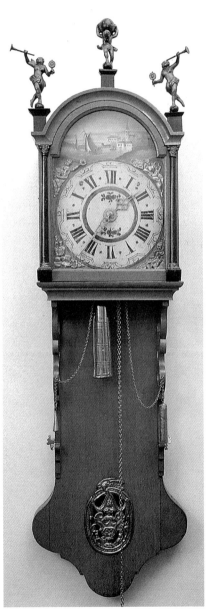

Above: Detail of a stoelklok, *c. 1800. A typical Dutch* stoelklok *features mermaids on either side at the back and cherubs on each side of the dial.*

Right: Staartklok, *c. 1840.* Staartkloks *of this style were made in Friesland in the first half of the 19th century. Note the top finials, with trumpeters and the figure of Atlas in the middle. ,*

providing a box to protect the pendulum. As on early longcase clocks, this box usually had a glazed aperture, which was often overlaid with decorative, fretted-out, gilded brass.

Early *staartkloks* tended to be fairly simple in concept, and the dials were again similar to those used on longcases of the same period. On later *staartkloks*, however, the dial was usually painted. Normally of thirty-hour duration, and employing exposed brass-cased weights, the majority of *staartkloks* are fairly large, usually with a seconds-beating pendulum. Smaller versions were nevertheless occasionally made. Varying appreciably were the finish of the cases: sometimes they were of simple oak, but sometimes they could be painted, carved or have marquetry let into them. And as with the *stoelklok*, strong regional variations rapidly developed.

HOODED WALL CLOCKS

The *staartklok* was a hooded wall clock. In England, the hooded wall clock was an attractive alternative to the lantern clock, but was produced only in limited numbers from the late 17th century to the end of the 18th century. The earlier examples usually had thirty-hour movements, with a single-handed brass dial anything from 5 inches (13cm) to 10 inches (25cm) square. In effect, these clocks rested on brackets, and were protected by a hood which slid off them. On London clocks, the hood may well have been veneered in mahogany or walnut, but on country clocks solid oak was the wood of choice.

As the century progressed, the breakarch dial came into fashion, while minute, and sometimes second, hands, were also provided. By 1780 the painted dial was being used, but by 1800 the production of hooded clocks in England had largely ceased.

THE TAVERN, OR ACT OF PARLIAMENT, CLOCK

By the reign of George II (reigned 1727–60), a highly efficient system of coaching existed over much of the country, making regular runs between the major cities and stopping to change horses and pick up passengers at the various coaching inns. Despite the weather, the condition of the roads and the ever-present fear of highwaymen (it was the era of robbers like the infamous Dick Turpin), the coaches kept surprisingly accurate time. It was, therefore, important for the inns also to have accurate clocks that were prominently displayed, and so the tavern clock was born.

Above: Act of Parliament clock by Thomas Bentley, Darlington, c. 1780. While the majority of tavern clocks had a circular dial and dropped trunk, other variants did exist, such as the shield shape or, as here, the teardrop.

Left: Hooded wall clock by John Ellicott, c. 1770. By the middle of the 18th century, the lantern clock was going out of fashion in favour of more decorative clocks, and one style that was to evolve was the hooded wall clock.

The terms 'tavern' and 'Act of Parliament' are, however, both terms that tend to be used synonymously to describe large, weight-driven wall clocks, usually with black lacquered cases. This usage, however, is incorrect, as tavern clocks were made from 1730 to 1735 onwards, while the Act of Parliament that gave the clocks their name was not introduced until 1797. The act imposed a duty of 5 shillings (25 pence) on every clock, 10 shillings (50 pence) on each gold watch, and 2 shillings and sixpence (12 pence) on those made of silver or other metals.

It is not surprising that most people seemed to have hidden their clocks and watches to avoid paying the duty, but the act did give rise to an increased number of large public clocks, usually tavern clocks, by which to tell the time. This helps to explain the alternative name of 'Act of Parliament' clocks. The act provoked such a disastrous decline in the demand for watches and clocks that clockmakers petitioned the government, and, within a year, the act was repealed.

Early tavern clocks usually have a square dial with a shallow arch at the top, following the curve of the chapter ring. Below the dial, there is the trunk into which the pendulum and weight extend. The basically square dial would eventually evolve into a shield shape, and octagonal dials were also used. The circular dial, in either white or black, made its appearance on these clocks in around 1760. By 1780–90, the use of the lacquered case had largely given way to mahogany, and within two decades their production had almost ceased.

DIAL CLOCKS

English cartel clocks, like their French cousins, but with cases of gilt wood rather than fire-gilt brass, started to appear around 1730, and then continued to be made for some 50 years, albeit in only small numbers.

These, and the circular black-dial clocks that started to be made around the same time, employed spring-driven movements with a verge escapement. In fact, this form of escapement was to continue on all spring-driven wall clocks until the end of the 18th century.

Some time after the black-dial clock was produced, white-dial clocks, still using a wooden background, became fashionable, but from the 1760s these were gradually replaced by engraved and silvered-brass dials, which were to remain in common use until the early 19th century. From 1780, however, the convex painted dial was also to become increasingly fashionable.

Around 1800, the decorative mahogany case became popular, and was usually employed with a drop trunk that either chamfered (chiselled back at 45 degrees) or, later, curved back towards the wall. As the Regency period progressed, decorative brass inlay was added, and by around 1830 there was often a glazed, brass-bound aperture in the front of the trunk through which the pendulum bob could be seen swinging to and fro. By the middle of the century, the convex dial had given way to a flat one.

Throughout the entire 19th century, and well into the 20th, the simple, circular, painted dial, spring-driven fusee wall clock was produced in very large numbers, and was used throughout the country in various public places, such as schools, railway stations, offices and in the home, in addition to being exported throughout the world.

THE VIENNA REGULATOR:
AUSTRIAN AND GERMAN WALL CLOCKS

The term 'Vienna regulator' is another confusing one, in that these clocks, which feature a movement with exposed brass-case

Left: Tavern clock by J Ireland, London, late 18th century. At the bottom of the trunk are the words which, translated, read 'Drink up or leave', a message obviously designed to stimulate turnover at the bar.

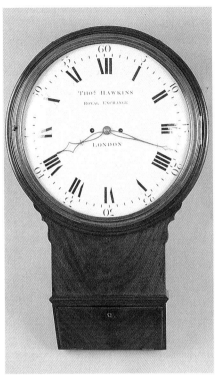

Left: Mahogany-cased wall clocks. Towards the end of the 18th century, lacquer decoration became unfashionable for the decoration of large clocks. In its place, mahogany was used.

Above: Silvered-dial wall clock, late 18th century. A direct descendent of the cartel clock, the English wall clock, with engraved and silvered-brass dial, probably started to appear around 1770. Nearly always simple timepieces without strike, many did, however have decorative engraving and beautifully executed signatures.

pendulum bob and usually weights within a fully glazed case, were not, in fact, always made in Vienna. To understand this, it must be remembered that from 1529 to 1918 Austria was part of the Austro-Hungarian Empire, and it is for this reason that clocks made in Austria, Hungary and the former Czechoslovakia, for example, often bearing striking similarities. Vienna was, however, undoubtedly the most important of the imperial courts, and consequently its influence on many areas of design and culture, including clocks, was the strongest.

During the late 17th century and for a large part of the 18th century, English clockmaking was to have a strong influence on Austrian

Above: Striking spring-driven wall clock by Thomas Hawkins, London c. 1800. Around the turn of the 19th century some very fine mahogany wall clocks were being produced. These had a trunk below the dial, with what is known as a chisel base, since it slopes back to a sharp point at the wall.

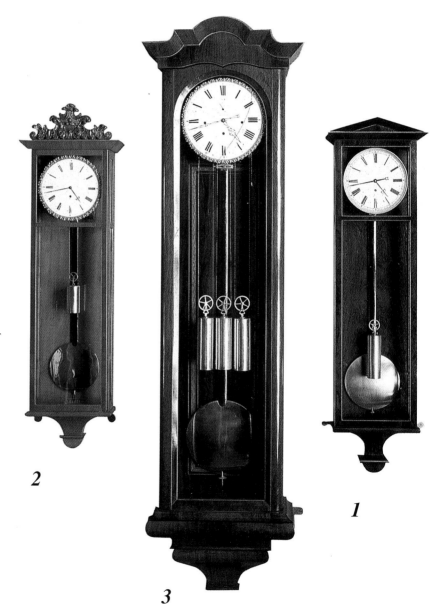

Above: Eight-day laterndluhr Vienna regulator by G J Bauer, c. 1830. The laterndluhr was almost the first style of case to appear in Vienna c. 1800. Roughly 5 feet (1.5m) long, it incorporated a seconds-beating pendulum. There were, however, smaller versions, even minatures at 20 inches (51cm) long.

Right: Vienna regulators, 1825–50.
1: *A dachluhr (roof-top case), which is also a six-light, as it is glazed with six pieces of glass, two on each side, which are divided by a glazing bar.*
2: *An eight-day cherrywood Vienna regulator, also with six-light case, and with pie-crust bezel around the dial.*
3: *A rare mahogany-cased wall clock of three-month duration, with* grande-sonnerie *striking on gongs, and a wood-rod pendulum.*

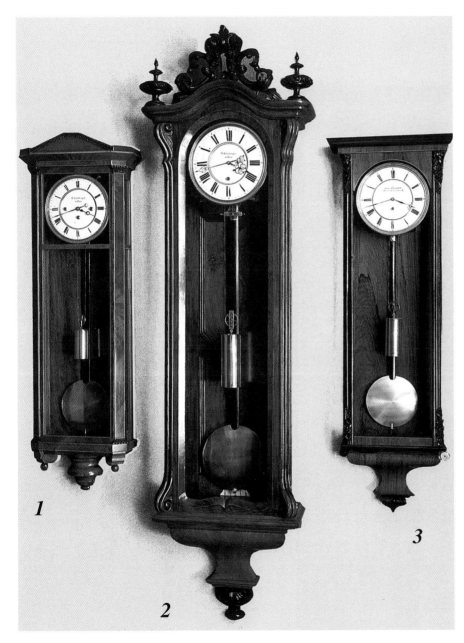

clockmaking, with designs being copied and movements – indeed whole clocks – being imported. In 1780, however, it was decided to improve the standard of Austria's clock- and watchmaking by inviting some 50 Swiss craftsmen – subsequently increased to 150 – to come and work there. Many of these craftsmen were specialists in, for example, dial, bezel, wheel, pinion and file manufacture, and no doubt the skills they taught their Austrian colleagues provided the foundations for the beautifully executed clocks made in the Austro-Hungarian Empire in the first half of the 19th century.

A second influence on the Viennese was that of the French, whose role as arbiters of European taste was reinforced by the marriage of Napoleon to Marie Louise of the house of Habsburg in 1804. This confluence gave rise to an increased interest in, and appreciation of, the classical proportions of classical art and architecture, and to the Vienna regulator, the perfect example of such classicism. However, there was a big difference between the French and Austro-Hungarian products, in that the latter were much more restrained and more delicately constructed than French examples. Undoubtedly, this made the Austro-Hungarian versions cheaper to produce and so more affordable, but it also made them far

Left: Two-piece dial clocks,
mid-19th century. The two-piece dial – with
recessed centre – had come into style in the
1840s.
1: A mahogany two-day clock from c. 1845.
2: A walnut clock of three-month duration,
with seconds-beating, signed by
Schonberger, c. 1855.
3:. A rosewood-veneered eight-day time-
piece. Note that all the veneers are laid so
that they run vertically.

less appealing in many people's eyes.

The years 1800 to 1860 are considered the golden age of Austrian clockmaking, for during this period the ingenuity of the clockmakers was, on many occasions, quite exceptional. Clocks were being produced with various types of compensated pendulums, complex calendar work and often of long duration – anything up to a year and even more was possible. Throughout this time, the number of clockmakers employed continued to increase, and it was only with the advent of mass-produced clocks – which were very similar in general appearance and were made in southern Germany from 1870 onwards by firms such as Gustav Becker, Junghans and Lenzkirch – that the Austrian clockmaking industry began its decline.

Although these later clocks were often of good quality, they cannot be compared with those clocks produced in the Biedermeier period in Vienna. On the German clocks, there is a minimum of hand-finishing, the hands are usually stamped out, and the dial bezels are of simple forms and spun up out of brass rather than cast.

As the end of the century approached, cases became far heavier, weighed down by what many would consider to be excessive ornamentation. At this time, spring-driven clocks,

Left: Austrian and German wall clocks, 19th century.
1: A simple eight-day mahogany Vienna timepiece.
2: An eight-day rosewood grande-sonnerie-striking *Viennese wall clock.*
3: Both the Viennese and Germans made some longcase clocks. Here is a German example, with a well-figured walnut case, c. 1880–90, with a key drawer in the base.

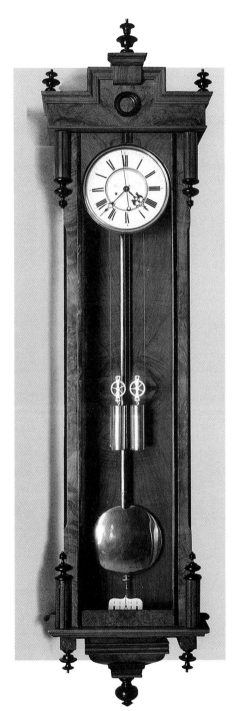

sometimes smaller than the standard size, began to appear. No doubt this was in part to reduce the cost of manufacture, an important factor at this time due to new, increased competition from American clocks.

AMERICAN SHELF AND WALL CLOCKS

Following the War of Independence in America, there was a shortage of materials and a rapidly growing demand for cheaper and smaller clocks than the longcase. Several clockmakers, backed up by the wealth of experience of immigrant clockmakers from such countries as England, The Netherlands and Germany, devised methods of fulfilling this demand by designing and making clock machinery that could be easily produced by factory techniques, as opposed to handcrafting production methods. Possibly the most famous of these clockmakers was Eli Terry (1772–1853), who, by 1810, had filled an order – the famous Porter Order – for some 4,000 complete clock movements at four dollars apiece over a period of three years.

Other makers involved in the early days of factory production were Seth Thomas, Chauncey Jerome and Simon Willard, the maker of the attractive 'banjo' clock, so called because of its resemblance in shape to the musical instrument. More clocks by Joshua Wilder (1786–1860) have survived than those made by any other clockmaker.

The early clocks were usually weight-driven timepieces, but by 1840 striking spring-driven clocks had been introduced, and many distinctive styles had evolved. The best-known group comprises shelf clocks, while other distinctive styles are the light-house clock by Simon Willard, the lyre clock (a more ornate form of the banjo clock), the acorn clock (where the dial is housed in an acorn-shaped

Left: Seconds-beating German wall regulator, late 19th century. This late-19th-century German 'full-length' walnut wall regulator features a wood-rod pendulum and a centre-sweep seconds hand.

Above: Black Forest wall clocks. This trio of wall clocks was made in the Black Forest area of Germany in the first half of the 19th century.

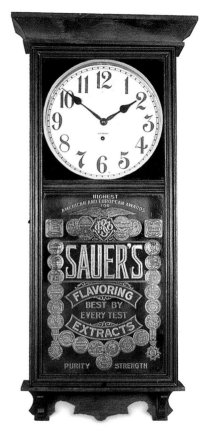

case), pillar and scroll clocks and both steeple and 'steeple on steeple' clocks. Also produced during this century were a considerable number of novelty clocks.

One of the most interesting clocks made at this time was the so-called 'wagon spring'. The term 'wagon spring' refers to the way in which the clock is driven: a large leaf spring at the base of the clock is flexed at either end to give the clock its motive power, and resembles the spring of a wagon. Its invention was brought about because at the time in the United States there was no manufacturing of coiled springs.

Another fascinating clock, which was first devised in the United States but subsequently gained world-wide popularity, was the torsion clock, which was invented by Aaron Crane. Its escapement was activated by the very slow winding and unwinding of a steel strip. This only required minimal power, and allowed for clocks of one-year duration to be made relatively easily. This invention in America gave rise in Europe to the production of 400-day or 'anniversary' clocks.

Triple-decker shelf clock, Dyer, Wadsworth and Company, Augusta, Georgia, c. 1835.

Advertising wall clock, Gilbert Clock Company, Winstead, Connecticut, c. 1920.

CARRIAGE AND SKELETON CLOCKS; MYSTERY AND FANTASY CLOCKS

Following the invention in around 1500 of the coiled spring to provide power, the travelling clock became a far more attractive proposition. Although portable, weight-driven clocks had been made, these were difficult to use, and a special box was required to keep the clock and the weights together. Each time the clock was moved, it had to be packed up and re-set in its new location by hanging it on the wall and adding the weights. With the new spring-driven clocks, none of these problems existed.

The most easily portable timekeeper is, of course, the watch, but this is for personal and not general use in a household. It is likely that the earliest travelling clocks made were those from southern Germany, such as the rectangular or hexagonal table clocks which often originally had travelling cases. Similar such clocks were also made in France and in Italy.

FRENCH CARRIAGE CLOCKS

Another form of travelling clock was the coach watch. This was, in fact, very similar to a giant watch, while in England small bracket clocks were also made with travelling cases. It was in France, however, that the major developments in travelling clocks took place.

Apart from the clock termed the *pendule de voyage*, two distinct styles evolved: one was the *pendule d'officier*, the other was the Capucine. Neither of these, however, were to enjoy a very long life, and they were eventually swept from the scene by the carriage clock.

The first carriage clocks were undoubtedly made by Abraham-Louis Breguet, but only in very small numbers. They were also very

Previous page: Swiss pendule d'officier, Robert & Courvoisier, Geneva, c. 1790.

Left: French Breguet carriage clock, No 5017, sold 1853.

expensive, and usually extremely complex clocks. Although the basic design of these was conceived in Breguet's lifetime, they went on being produced long after his death. In fact, many of the later pieces made in the last part of the 19th century and the beginning of the 20th century were 'bought-in' pieces, to which Breguet merely added his own name then and retailed them.

The first clockmaker to produce carriage

Above: French multi-piece carriage clock, c. 1835. A relatively early example of a French carriage clock, this has a two-train movement, striking and repeating on a gong.

Left: French Garnier carriage clock, No 3697, 1845. A finely engraved, but comparatively late, example of the work of Paul Garnier.

Above: Case styles. Many different styles of clock case, including corniche (top left and centre), cannelee (bottom left), gorge (bottom centre) and doucine (serpentine fronted, top row, right) evolved during the second half of the 19th century.

Right: Case sizes. The extreme range of sizes of carriage clocks, from the giant English example at 10.5 inches (27cm) high down to the subminiature Swiss carriage clock, with its enamelled panels, is shown here.

clocks in any quantity was Paul Garnier (1801–69), and he usually employed his own form of escapement, the chaffcutter. By the late 1830s, Garnier had been joined by other makers, such as Bolviller, Auguste, Jules, Berolla and Lepine, and by the 1850s carriage-clock production was in full swing, with all the benefits that mass production could bring.

Many different styles of clock case evolved, mostly during the second half of the 19th century, as well as an extreme range of sizes. In addition to giant, some 10.5 inches (27cm) high, there was full size (between 4.5 inches (11.4cm) and 6.5 inches (16.5cm) in height), miniature (*c*. 3 inches (6.2cm) high) and sub-miniature, at a mere *c*, 2 inches (3.7cm) in height, excluding the handle.

As the century progressed, the market expanded, and some of the best-known makers were Drocourt, Couaillet, Dumas, Duverdrey & Bloquel, Jacot, Japy Freres, Lamaille, Henry Marc, Margaine, Maurice, Pons, Richard & Cie and Soldano. It is difficult, however, to know precisely in what quantities they all made their clocks, since the majority are unsigned: the retailers preferred to have only their own name on the dial.

In order to make the carriage clocks more appealing, various types of decoration were introduced. The most common decoration was engraving, which varied both in extent and in quality. Other methods of decorating clocks included substituting glass panels and plain white dials with decorative porcelain panels, often bearing a romantic scene. Another popular form of ornamentation was *champlevé* enamelling, where the enamel is fused onto the incised or hollow areas of the metal base. Enamelled panels, usually from Limoges, were also used, as were those decorated with multicoloured gold and silver.

Carriage-clock production continued at a relatively high level until the outbreak of World War I in 1914, and although production recommenced in 1918, far fewer clocks were produced, and their output continued to decrease until by 1939 it was very small. Nevertheless, carriage clocks continued to be made, and today probably more carriage clocks are produced than in the past 40 years. Several firms are now involved, including some in England, and one company, L'Epee, in Sainte-Suzanne, which made carriage clocks over a century ago, continues to do so today.

ENGLISH CARRIAGE CLOCKS

Although carriage clocks started to be made in England at around the same time as they

Above and above right: English engraved carriage clock, c. 1850. A superbly cast, chased and engraved carriage-clock case, *with columns at the four corners, engraved side panels with heraldic beasts, and, on the back, a basket of flowers.*

were in France, no serious attempt was made to compete with the French carriage-clock industry. The clocks made in England were usually far larger, heavier and much more expensive to manufacture. In England, almost the exact opposite approach to the French seems to have been adopted: many carriage

Below left: French porcelain-panelled gorge-cased carriage clock by Drocourt, 1880. Panels of Sèvres enamel, all with blue grounds and decorated with beads of semi-precious stones and pearls, depict country scenes, with cottages, trees, flowers and a lake.

Below right: French champlevé-enamelled carriage clock, c. 1890. A popular form of decoration applied to metalwork in France in the last half of the 19th century was multi-coloured champlevé enamelling. Recesses are cut into brass and then filled with different colours of enamel that are fired individually at high temperatures.

clocks were still using chain fusees, and they were apparently often made with little regard as to expense, incorporating such features as a chronometer escapement. When a travelling case was provided, in England it was usually of wood, unlike the French leather cases. Whereas in France there was a relatively large number of manufacturers, in England, production of carriage clocks was largely confined to a few top names: McCabe, Frodsham, Dent, Vulliamy, Barwise, Smith and Jump.

As a viable alternative to the French carriage clock, a few small English carriage timepieces were made with a going barrel (no fusee) and without strike. These clocks usually had solid sides and a back door, and do not appear to have been a success.

SWISS CARRIAGE CLOCKS

The Swiss produced a limited number of carriage clocks similar to those made in the Franche-Comté region of eastern France in the earlier period. Two of the most famous makers were Frederic and Auguste Courvoisier, but it is likely that the majority of the later carriage clocks bearing Swiss names were made either wholly, or in part, in France. However, from around 1900 to 1930, an attractive range of miniature Swiss carriage clocks were produced around Geneva by firms such as the Geneva Clock Company. These were usually beautifully decorated with coloured enamels, and were retailed by leading firms like Cartier and Asprey.

AUSTRIAN CARRIAGE CLOCKS

The Viennese produced a most attractive series of travelling/carriage clocks between 1800 and 1850. These usually had engine-turned, fire-gilt cases, sometimes glazed at the sides, and had movements of two-day duration. Frequently

Above: Austrian carriage clock by Michael Gruebmullner, c. 1800–10. Between 1800 and 1850 the Austrians produced carriage clocks that were entirely different from the French models. They were nearly always of two-day duration, and had grande-sonnerie striking, with an alarm.

Right inset: French skeleton clock by Verneuil, late 18th century. With its strong Egyptian motifs, this clock was no doubt inspired by Napoleon's victories at around that time.

Right: French glass-plated skeleton clock, c. 1800. With the wheelwork apparently suspended in mid-air– there being no visible frame – this is undoubtedly the ultimate in skeleton-clock design and execution.

these clocks also incorporated a duplex escapement and struck the quarters on bells, but more commonly on gongs.

AMERICAN CARRIAGE CLOCKS

A few American firms mass produced carriage clocks, usually of a relatively simple design, and sometimes copying those produced in France. In other instances, American clockmakers devised their own distinctive styles.

The Waterbury Clock Company undoubtedly made a large number of carriage clocks, but they were also manufactured by the Ansonia Clock Company, Chauncey Jerome, Seth Thomas, the Boston Clock Company and the Vermont Clock Company.

SKELETON CLOCKS

The skeleton clock was devised to display the clockmaker's skill and ingenuity as completely as possible. To that end, no case was provided, simply a protective glass dome or a glazed brass frame. Frequently, the dial was fretted out and its centre omitted, and on English clocks in particular, the movement plates were also fretted out.

The design of the clock gradually evolved in the last half of the 18th century from the fine *pendules de cheminée* being made in France. This was a time of great wealth and patronage of the arts and sciences – albeit on the part of a small number of people. They demanded the best, and happily this coincided with the greatest period in French horology, with superb makers such as Janvier, Berthoud, Lepine, the Lepautes, Bailly and Breguet arriving on the scene.

FRENCH SKELETON CLOCKS

Up until around 1800, French skeleton clocks all tended to be different, and they were often

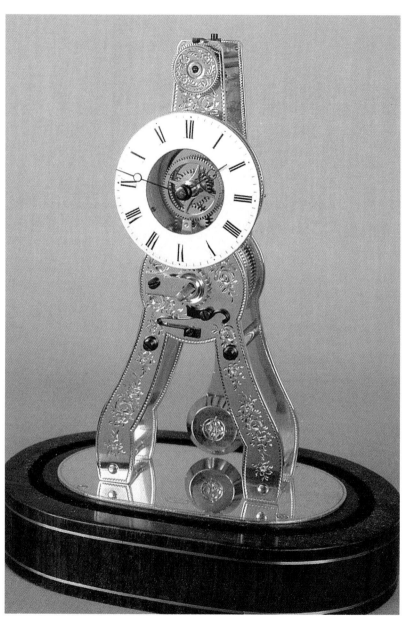

also very complex, employing, for instance, a *remontoir*. This was a device for converting a spring-driven clock into a weight-driven one by using the mainspring to wind up a small weight at regular, short intervals. This provided even more power than a spring, and greatly improved the timekeeping.

Other additional features added to the clocks at this time included the moon's age and phases, simple and perpetual-calendar work, and an additional hand so that mean time (our time) and solar time were shown, as well as the 'equation of time' – the difference between our time and that shown on a sundial.

After 1810, although fascinating one-off clocks continued to be produced, certain standard designs were also adopted and made, although in very small numbers. Examples of these include beautiful glass-plated clocks, possibly the ultimate in skeleton-clock design, which often run for six months on one winding. A similar, but keyhole-framed, design was also produced, and Verneuil made a series of fine, often quite large, calendar skeleton clocks.

But one of the best-known examples of a French skeleton clock was the one shown at the Crystal Palace in the 1851 Great Exhibition in London's Hyde Park. At only 10 inches (25.4cm) tall, it was produced over a long period in appreciable numbers and in several different forms.

AUSTRIAN SKELETON CLOCKS
The primary manufacturing base of skeleton clocks in the Austro-Hungarian Empire

French Great Exhibition skeleton clock by Victor Pierret, mid-19th century. These clocks were so called because they were exhibited and sold in great numbers at the Great Exhibition of 1851 at the Crystal Palace.

Above: Viennese skeleton clock, c. 1820–30.
This attractive Viennese skeleton clock is of
eight-day duration, and has a fine driving
weight decorated with engine turning.

Above: Austrian skeleton clock, mid-19th
century. This clock epitomises the gaiety
and fun of mid-century Vienna, with its
ornate, wooden frame decorated with
gold leaf and smothered with silver
repoussé work.

was concentrated in Vienna and began in around 1800. Strongly influenced by French models, the Austrian clocks nevertheless rapidly assumed their own individuality, and many of the early examples were of considerable complexity and ingenuity. For example, a few were weight driven, but the later pieces tended to be fairly standard-ised and spring driven, of two-day dura-tion and quarter striking.

ENGLISH SKELETON CLOCKS

Skeleton-clock manufacture began in England in around 1820, and the early examples made use of French styles, usually employing an inverted Y-shaped frame. Although few such clocks were made prior to 1835, after this time production escalated, no doubt encouraged by the momentum of the Industrial Revolution. By 1850–60, the numbers of skeleton clocks being made in England vastly outnumbered those made in France and Austria.

One of the first of what might be called pure-ly English design was the simple Gothic frame,

Left: English skeleton clock, c. 1825. A typical example of an English skeleton clock, this model features the inverted Y-frame which was also popular with French makers at the same time.

Above: English Gothic-frame skeleton clock, c. 1840. The simple Gothic frame fol-lowed close on the heels of the inverted Y-frame, and was used mainly between 1835 and 1850, after which time it tended to be replaced by architectural clocks.

Right: Group of English skeleton clocks, mid-19th century.

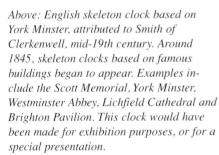

Above: English skeleton clock based on York Minster, attributed to Smith of Clerkenwell, mid-19th century. Around 1845, skeleton clocks based on famous buildings began to appear. Examples include the Scott Memorial, York Minster, Westminster Abbey, Lichfield Cathedral and Brighton Pavilion. This clock would have been made for exhibition purposes, or for a special presentation.

usually only 11–12 inches (28–30.5cm) tall, and generally just a timepiece. This was quickly followed by the scroll frame which was produced first by Edwards of Stourbridge.

Subsequently, there was a rapid increase in the range of clocks available, and even musical versions were offered. The variety of frames was also extended to include those based on famous buildings such as Lichfield Cathedral, York Minster and Brighton Pavilion. Floral designs were also produced that incorporated fuchsias and ivy leaves.

The vast majority of English skeleton clocks were produced by a few specialist manufacturers, such as Evans of Handsworth in Birmingham and Smith of Clerkenwell in London. But there were some other clockmakers who, although they made a relatively small number of skeleton clocks, produced some superb-quality and ingenious pieces. Examples that spring to mind are Pace's and James Condliff's clocks, which frequently employed a seconds-beating balance. By 1890, however, the heyday of English skeleton clocks was over, and 20 years later only a handful of simple timepieces were being produced.

MYSTERY, NOVELTY AND FANTASY CLOCKS

As their names imply, these clocks are designed not simply to tell the time, but to fascinate in one way or another, by perhaps mystifying the viewer, or amusing them with automata (moving figures) that perform either when the clock is running or when it strikes.

The first of these clocks originated in southern Germany in the 17th century. Clocks were produced in the form of animals and people whose eyes moved in time with the pendulum. Others were far more complex: arms, legs, heads and necks might move, imitating an action such as eating. One of the most fascinating is the Chariot Clock in the Time Museum, in Rockford, Illinois, which shows the gluttonous, mythical King Gambrinus sitting on a chariot. As the chariot gradually proceeds down the dining table under its own power, the king raises a tankard in his right hand to his mouth, which, at the same time, opens and closes as though he is drinking.

In the 19th century the French produced a series of clocks designed to mystify everyone regarding how they worked. There is no apparent movement behind the dial, for example, nor do the hands mounted on the glass dial appear to have any possible means of driving them; or the movement, which is situated in the base, is separated from the dial by a glass column, thereby suggesting that there is no means of connection. Many of these fine clocks were made by the brilliant illusionist Robert Houdin in around 1840 to 1860. Some fine automata were also made with tightrope

English skeleton clock by James Condliff, c. 1840. Condliff was undoubtedly one of the finest – if not the finest – English skeleton clockmakers, and this is a typical example of his work.

walkers and jugglers. Another fascinating clock from this period is one where the hours and minutes are indicated by the rise and fall of a girl's arms.

Meanwhile, the blinking-eye clocks which originated in Augsburg in the 17th century were produced in simplified form in southern Germany in the mid-19th century, as well as in the United States. The American versions were nearly always made in cast iron, and were

Above: French mystery clock, c. 1850.
A fascinating and beautifully executed
French mystery clock, in which the dial has
no apparent connection with the movement.

Left and below:
Gambrinus Chariot
Clock, c. 1600.
Many complex clocks,
which often incorpo-
rated automata (mov-
ing parts), were made
in Augsburg during the
16th and 17th cen-
turies. Depicted here is
the gluttonous, mythi-
cal King Gambrinus,
who is associated with
brewing. Either on the
hour, or when activat-
ed, the clock proceeds
down the table. As it
does so, the king
raises and lowers his
hand, which contains a
mug of beer, and at the
same time opens and
closes his mouth.

in the form of minstrels, dogs or lions.

A further ingenious series of clocks was made in France from around 1880 to 1910. These were mostly associated with aspects of the Industrial Revolution, and were always of fine quality. They showed, for example, a steam hammer or a beam engine at work, or a lighthouse revolving.

Right: John Bull blinking-eye clock, Bradley and Hubbard Manufacturing Co, Connecticut, c. 1860.

Below left: French mystery clock, 1865. Below right: Glass-dialled mystery clock, Robert Houdin, c. 1845.